JAZZ
FOR GUITAR

by PAT MARTINO

PHILOSOPHY

The philosophy of the REH HOTLINE SERIES is to give you a larger and varied vocabulary of licks and melodic ideas. Many guitarists want to have their own original style and feel they shouldn't copy licks from other players. In reality, it is a proven fact by most top 'original' players that it is very beneficial, if not necessary, to study other players, learn their ideas, phrasing, etc. Some of the benefits of learning such lines are: Developing the ear - by playing and singing these lines you will soon 'hear' and understand melodies and how they relate to chords; Building technique and confidence - the Hotlines are great for building chops and will also give you an arsenal of ideas to fall back on; Music theory - an understanding of improvising theory can be gained by learning and analyzing the lines which are built from scales, arpeggios and intervals.

Here are some suggestions to help you get the most out of the Hotlines:

- Play them in all keys and, if possible, in different octaves.

- Since many of the lines are written in simple 16th notes for quick ic̲ breaking them up rhythmically (syncopating) or phrasing them in different parts oɪ ṯḥ̲

- Feel free to add effects like: Hammer-ons, Pull-offs, slurs and bends.

- Experiment with the lines over chords different from the ones suggested.

- Although the author's fingerings and positions are shown for each of the Hotlines, you may want to make some adjustments to make them more comfortable.

- The last and most important thing is to work the lines, in whole or in part, into your playing right away.

PLAYBACK+
Speed • Pitch • Balance • Loop

To access audio, visit:
www.halleonard.com/mylibrary

Enter Code
4884-1967-1130-5382

Cover Photo by William Hames

ISBN 978-1-61774-193-7

HAL•LEONARD®

Visit Hal Leonard Online at
www.halleonard.com

Contact us:
Hal Leonard
7777 West Bluemound Road
Milwaukee, WI 53213
Email: info@halleonard.com

In Europe, contact:
Hal Leonard Europe Limited
42 Wigmore Street
Marylebone, London, W1U 2RN
Email: info@halleonardeurope.com

In Australia, contact:
Hal Leonard Australia Pty. Ltd.
4 Lentara Court
Cheltenham, Victoria, 3192 Australia
Email: info@halleonard.com.au

HOTLINE # 1

The first line works over a II-V-I chord progression in the key of C major. Note the use of passing tones and arpeggiated chord shapes throughout. Notice in bar #2 the third & fourth beats outline a Fmaj7 arpeggio resolving chromatically to a G augmented arpeggio creating the sound of a G7#5 chord.

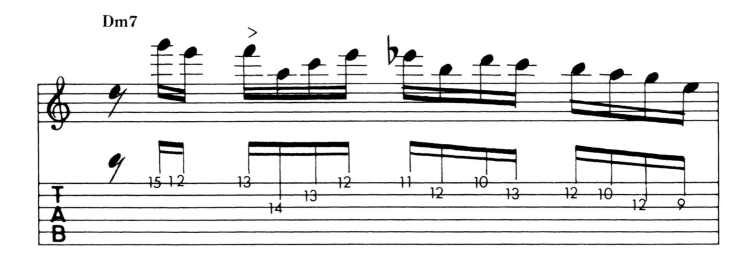

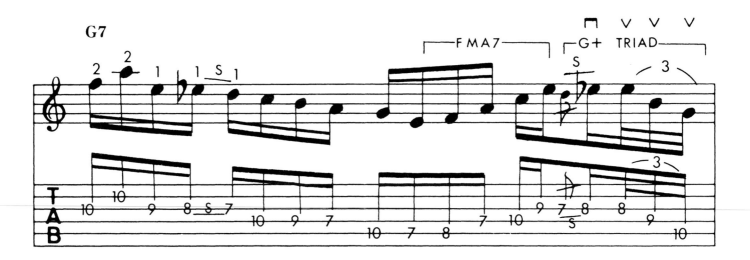

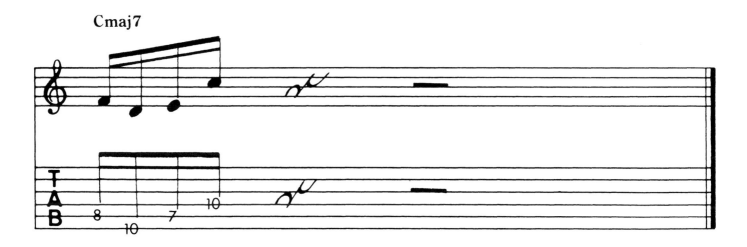

HOTLINE # 2

The second hotline works over a II-V-I chord progression in the key of G major. It incorporates an "A" melodic minor idea in the first bar (note the F# and G# notes). Bar #2 moves from A minor to D7 (note the D7#5 arpeggio on the third beat). The line resolves to a Gmaj7 chord by way of a small phrase accentuating the tones D, C, and Eb (the root flat seventh, and flat ninth of the D7 chord).

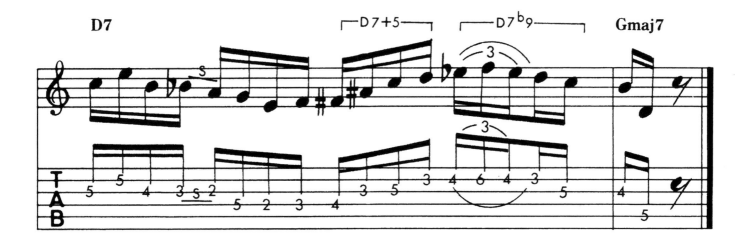

3

HOTLINE # 3

This hotline starts with a sequential pattern outlining "C" minor to "G" minor over the II chord of Bb major (Cm7). On the fourth beat of the first bar, an Ebmaj7 (Cm9) arpeggio is introduced and continues into the second bar (F7). In bar #2 beats three and four, an F7#5 to F7b9 sound is used. The line resolves to a "D" and "C" note, creating the sound of a Bbmaj9 chord. In bar #1, the opening pattern is played with the 3rd, 4th, and 1st fingers respectively. The same pattern is played on the 2nd, 3rd, and 4th strings again.

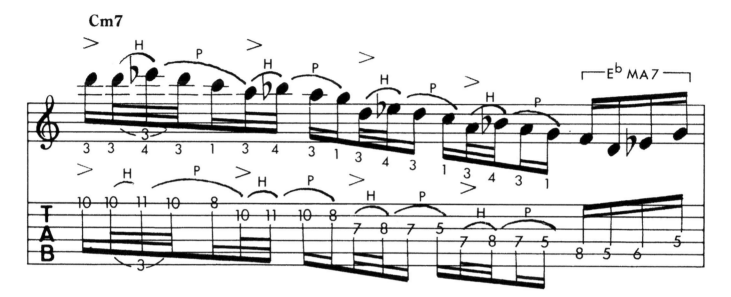

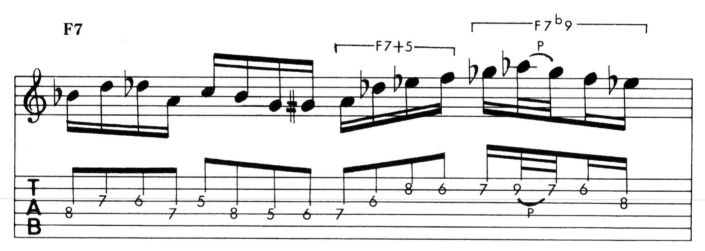

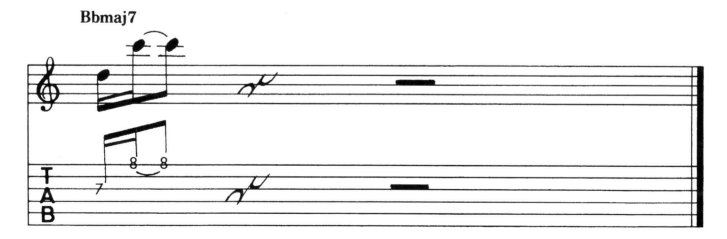

HOTLINE # 4

Here we have a II-V-I in the key of C major. Bar #1 displays a descending melodic idea in the "D" dorian mode (2nd mode of C major). The D minor sets up an Abmaj6 arpeggio in bar #2 on the third beat, creating the sound of a G7(b9#5) chord. It then resolves to a Cmaj7 with the use of a simple diad anticipated at the end of bar #2.

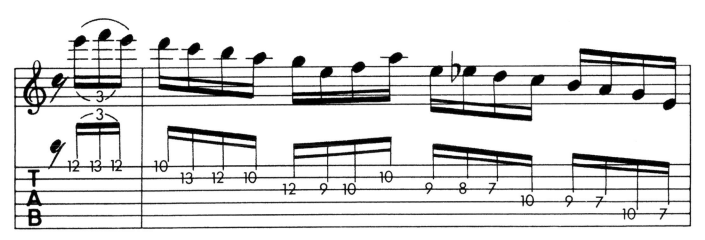

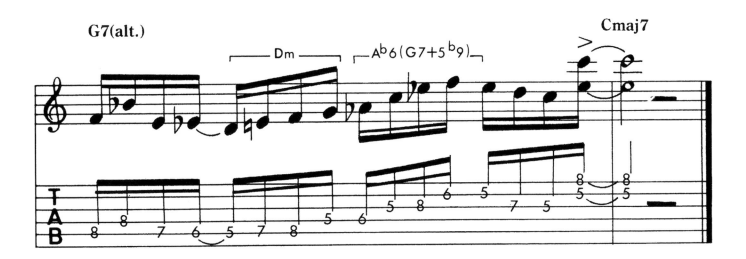

HOTLINE # 5

This hotline is a II-V-I in the key of G minor. It consists of a Cm7 idea in bar #1 (note the rhythmical variation on the Cm7 arpeggio on beats 1 & 2). Bar #2 introduces a more sophisticated rhythmical pattern comprised of descending dominant seventh arpeggios. The concept here is that the listeners ear is focusing on the rhythmical movement rather than the melodic content of the musical phrase. The line resolves to Gm9 by way of an Ab dominant 7th arpeggio (tritone substitution).

Am7b5

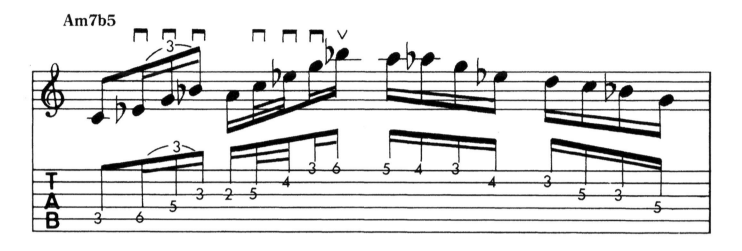

D7(alt.)

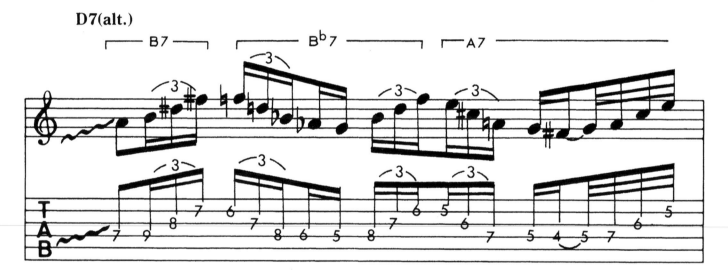

Gm7

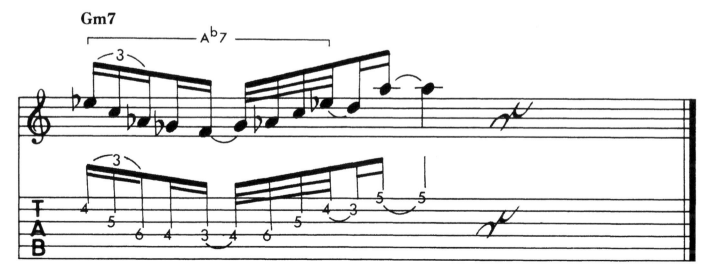

HOTLINE # 6

Hotline #6 is a II-V-I in the key of E minor. It utilizes a chromatic scale dispersed in octaves, ascending from a "B" note (in the 1st bar, 1st beat) to a "B" note two octaves up (2nd bar, down beat of 3). The upbeat of three starts a chromatic movement down, and resolves itself to a "G" note setting up an E minor arpeggio ending on the open E. Because of the chromatic nature of this pattern, it will fit over many other harmonic situations. Experiment and try to use this idea in other contexts. Also, this pattern is great for developing right and left hand co-ordination.

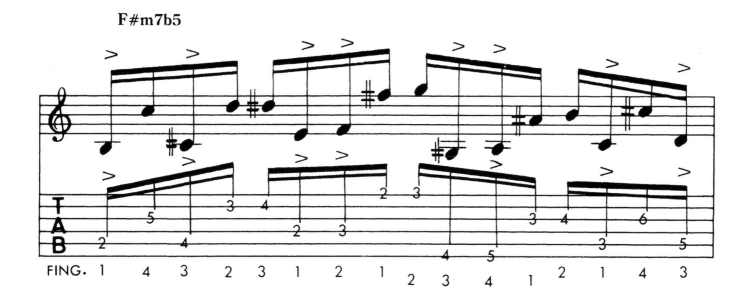

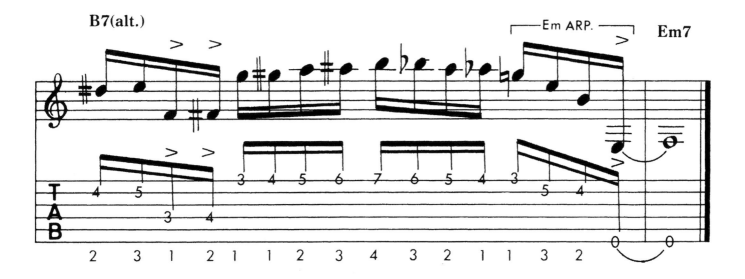

HOTLINE # 7

Try this hotline over an A minor chord. It begins as a scalar sequence in "A" melodic minor then converts to an "A" dorian mode (2nd mode of G major). This line can be used over many static (one chord) situations (ie. Am, Cmaj, D7 etc).

Am7

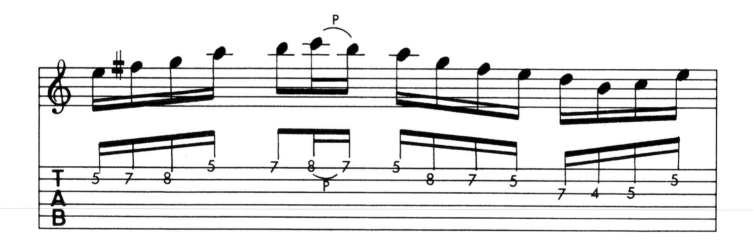

HOTLINE # 8

This line works over a C7 chord. Notice the ascending melodic line (a "C" blues scale) under the "C" note (tonic) in the upper voice. This "oblique motion" creates a very definite "Blues" flavor. The motif shifts an octave lower by way of a triadic type rhythmical phrase (bar 1, beat 3). Pay close attention to the special fingering and picking notations above and below the written music. These will assist you in performing the "Hotline" properly.

C7

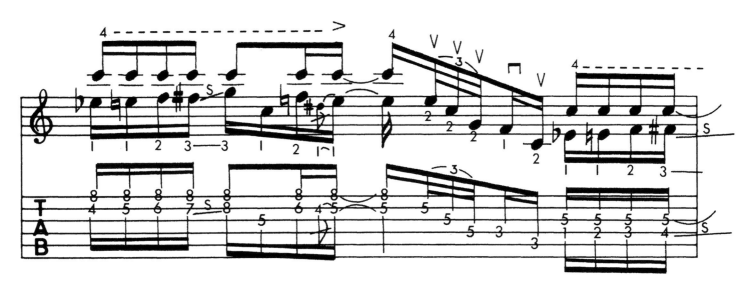

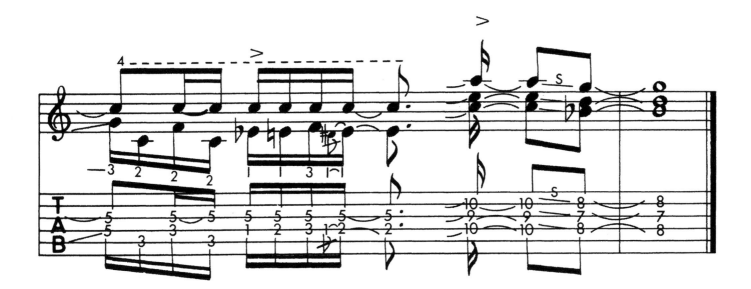

HOTLINE # 9

Hotline #9 is a more linear approach to playing over a C7 chord (as opposed to Hotline #8 which is more of a harmonic device). Notice that even though the bar harmony is a C7 chord, a G minor (Bb major) idea is used. When playing over a Dominant 7th chord, go up a P5 (perfect 5th) from the root of the dominant and play minor or, go down a M2 (major 2nd) from the root of the dominant and play major. Refer to Pat Martino "Linear Expressions" REH Publications.

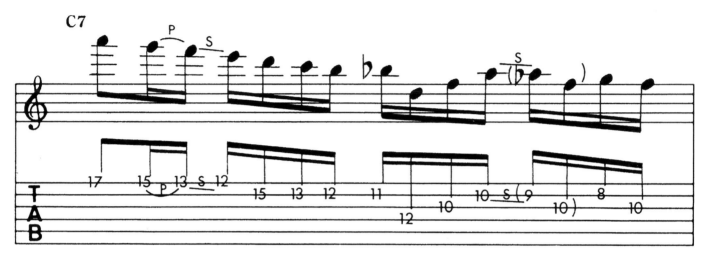

HOTLINE #10

This Hotline is an abbreviated version of "I Got Rhythm" changes. Note the G7#5b9 arpeggio at the end if bar #1. In bar #2, Cmaj7 moves to F7. Note the use of "F" pentatonic at the end of the bar. The line ends with a IIIm7, VI7, IIm7, V7 turn around into Bbmaj7.

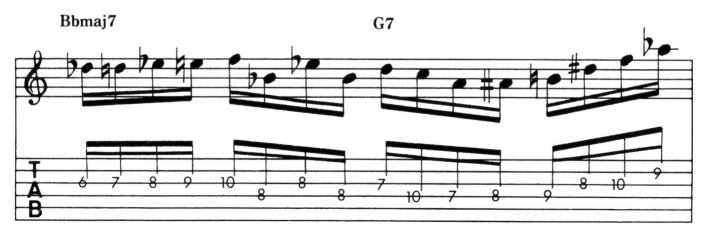

HOTLINE #10 (cont.)

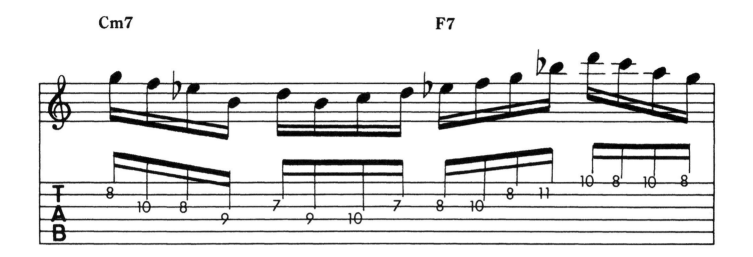

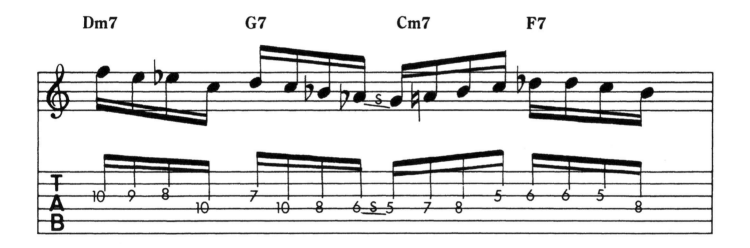

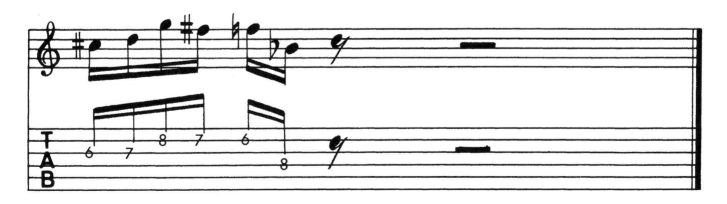

HOTLINE #11

Here we have a I, VI, II, V, I in the key of G major. Notice the use of Bm7 and Gmaj7 arpeggios in the first bar. Bar #2 utilizes Gmaj (Em) in moving to G7b9 phrase, setting up a Cmaj7 (Am) arpeggio at the beginning of bar #3. In bar #4, D7 moves to an F#m7b5 arpeggio resolving to Gmaj in bar #5 (F#m7b5 is a direct substitute chord for D7, creating the sound of a "D" dominant 9th chord). Substitutions are dealt with in more detail in the Pat Martino "Linear Expressions" book.

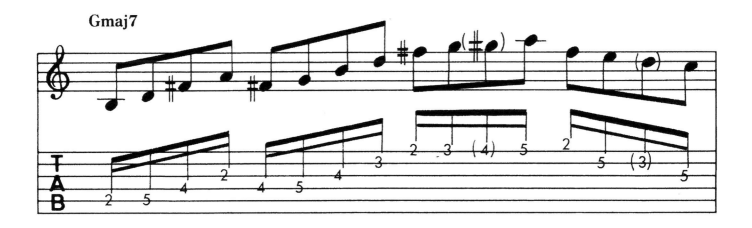

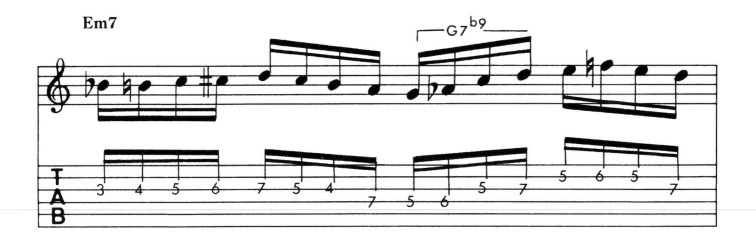

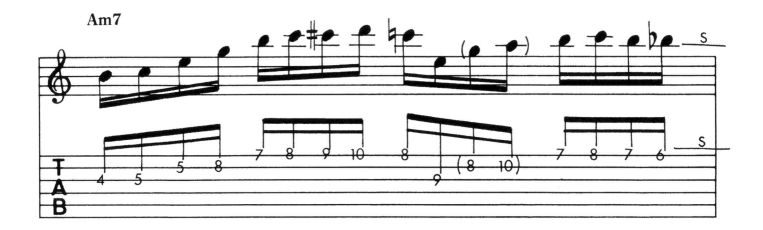

HOTLINE #11 (cont.)

HOTLINE #12

This Hotline illustrates a single motif which moves in a cycle of 4ths on the same set of strings. You may want to refer to Hotline #8 for fingering tips.

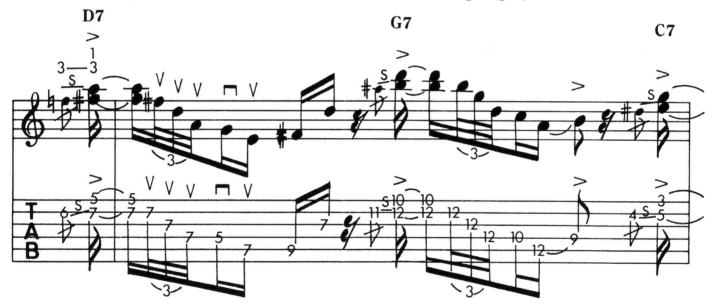

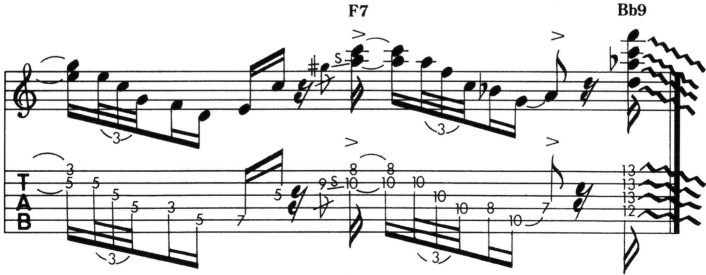

HOTLINE #13

This is a line for a III, VI, II, V, I in the key of G major. The line begins with a rhythmical phrase played on the first string with the first and third fingers and moves down chromatically. Note the use of chromatic passing tones in creating smooth movement through the chord changes, and the D7#9b5 arpeggio in bar #2 moving to an Ebm (D7 alt.).

Bm7

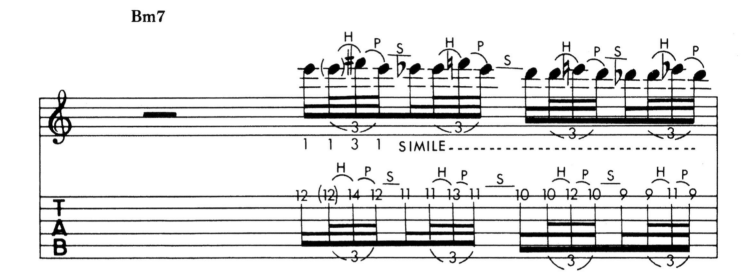

Em7

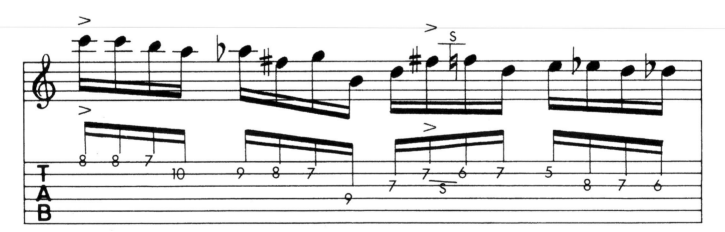

Am7

D7(alt.)

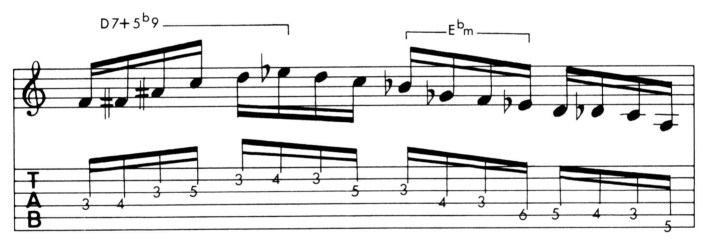

Gmaj7

HOTLINE #14

The last Hotline works over a VI, II, V, I chord progression in the key of Ab major. Again, the emphasis is on melodic movement. Note the line contour (alternating direction of the line). Also, this line could be used over the first four bars of the tune "All The Things You Are" by Jerome Kern.

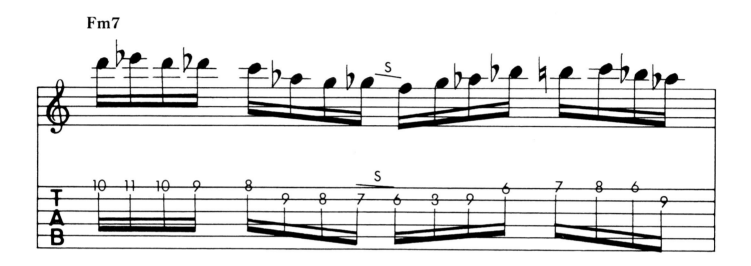